Original title:
Maybe Life Doesn't Have a Meaning... But I'm Still Here

Copyright © 2025 Creative Arts Management OÜ
All rights reserved.

Author: Aidan Marlowe
ISBN HARDBACK: 978-1-80566-066-8
ISBN PAPERBACK: 978-1-80566-361-4

The Whisper of an Unsung Song

In a world that spins like a dizzy top,
I juggle my dreams while my coffee won't stop.
Each moment a riddle, a giggle, a sigh,
I dance with the chaos and just let it fly.

With socks that don't match and hair like a nest,
I tackle my mornings in a comical quest.
An existential crisis in a cereal bowl,
I laugh at the questions, they tickle my soul.

The socks on the line sing a mocking refrain,
While I trip on my thoughts like a clumsy refrain.
The clouds in the sky wear a whimsical grin,
As I wade through the nonsense, embracing my spin.

So here I am grinning, with nothing to prove,
In the rhythm of life, I just go with the groove.
With jokes on my lips and a heart full of cheer,
I find joy in the murmur, I embrace the absurd here.

The Faint Glow of Uncertainty

In shadows where questions twirl,
I dance with doubts in a silly swirl.
The sun might hide, but I wear shades,
On this wild ride, confusion parades.

With each step, I trip over thoughts,
Like a lost duck in a field of knots.
Giggles echo in the quiet night,
As I chase sparkles that tease my sight.

When the Clock Ticks Yet Life Stills

Tick-tock goes the clock on the wall,
While I aim for the great, I end up small.
A marathon runner at a snail's pace,
Curiosity wears a goofy face.

Time flies by, I give it a wave,
But I'm stuck here, a sloth in a cave.
Grinning through each awkward event,
Where moments linger, my time is spent.

In Pursuit of the Unfathomable

I chase mirages like a kid with a kite,
While scoffing at the stars in the night.
Maybe wisdom's just a funky hat,
With jester bells on, imagine that!

Every "why" is a puzzled grin,
As I spin circles where thoughts have been.
In the maze where answers are rare,
Dancing with questions without a care.

Days Wrapped in Ambivalence

One day I'm high, the next I'm low,
Like a see-saw ride with nowhere to go.
Eating snacks of both doubt and cheer,
Life's a buffet, but I'm still here.

Wrapped in layers of what might be,
Like a burrito – fluffy, carefree.
Each fumble and stumble's a laugh in disguise,
With silly surprises in every guise.

Reflections in a Broken Mirror

A mirror cracked, I see my face,
It grins back at me, with all its grace.
I laugh at the bits that don't quite match,
Like my socks, which seem to hatch.

In this world of mix and blend,
Who said we need a perfect trend?
I'm here with quirks, a silly cheer,
Craziness blooms, like flowers, I steer.

Footsteps on an Unmarked Path

I wander off the paved main road,
Finding treasures in the weirdest load.
Each step may seem a bit unsure,
But hey, at least I've got allure!

With every rock and sudden bend,
I trip and laugh, call it my friend.
Who needs a map when you can roam?
The biggest joy is called 'unknown'!

Navigating the Unknown

A compass spins, it doesn't know,
Which way to go, fast or slow?
I pick a side and hop on by,
Like a squirrel chasing after pie.

The stars above, they seem to wink,
"Just sail along, don't you think?"
With every turn, I flip and twirl,
Oh look, I found another pearl!

The Colors of Uncertainty

A palette bright, a splash of doubt,
I paint my day, no need to pout.
With reds and blues, I swirl around,
In this wild, chaotic playground.

Each brushstroke brings a chuckle, too,
Life's a canvas, paint it blue!
I'll throw some green and purple spritz,
Who cares if it's all a bit of blitz?

Moments that Slip Away

A sandwich dropped on the floor,
A sock that runs far from me.
Time flies like a dog on a spree,
Chasing its tail, oh what a score!

I lost my keys but found my hat,
The fridge light buzzes, sings a tune.
I ponder life under the moon,
While searching for my lost cat.

The Weight of Unanswered Queries

Why does toast always land jam-side down?
Why do socks vanish without a trace?
I ponder these in a sleepy daze,
While wearing a shirt with a frown.

The questions stack like pancakes high,
When did laundry become such a chore?
Yet here I am, wanting more,
Flipping through life like a pie.

Heartbeats in a Void

A heartbeat laughs in the empty space,
Echoes of thoughts dance in my head.
I talk to myself, but just instead,
Of finding wisdom, I trip on grace.

The clock ticks slow, like honey spills,
Counting the seconds, what a game!
I smile because it feels the same,
As dancing alone on the windowsills.

A Symphony of Inconsequence

The rhythm of life plays off-key,
With hiccups and stumbles in tow.
I laugh at the things I don't know,
Like if squirrels can hear the sea.

So here I waltz in my mismatched shoes,
Doubling down on the silly and fun.
In this great play, I've already won,
With every giggle, I'm never to lose.

The Night is Heavy with Void

The moon's a big cheese, round and wide,
A cosmic joke played on this ride.
The stars giggle softly, just out of reach,
While I wander around like a puzzled peach.

The darkness yawns, stretching its limbs,
As I try to find meaning in life's silly whims.
A comet zooms past with a wink of its tail,
Leaving me here with a laugh and a tale.

A Milestone on an Undefined Path

I bought a map but it's upside down,
Got lost in a forest filled with a frown.
Each step I take on this twisted way,
Has me wondering what's for dinner today.

A signpost points, but it's in Greek,
I'm just trying to find a snack, so to speak.
The trees are just giggling at my plight,
While I hop from one puzzle to late-night bite.

Finding Serenity in the Unknown

In the chaos, I sip my herbal tea,
Wondering who put the 'wild' in 'wild and free?'
Beneath the stars, I ponder in glee,
Is there a punchline to this cosmic spree?

Breath in deep—ah, the unknown smells nice,
Like burnt popcorn and vanilla ice.
As serenity dances like a flexible cat,
I just hope it saves me a seat on the mat.

Stars That Yearn to be Found

Stars seem to wink, as if they know,
That I'm stumbling through life, putting on a show.
They're like my audience, a sparkling crowd,
Cheering me on, though I'm not feeling proud.

The skies hum a melody, silly and bright,
Dancing like fireflies in the soft night light.
If I trip on my shoelaces while dreaming out loud,
I just hope those stars throw me a cloud.

Breathing in the Paradox

I dance with shadows in the light,
Chasing laughter; it feels so right,
Juggling thoughts like a circus clown,
With a big red nose, I won't back down.

The world spins madly, what a show,
Finding joy in the highs and lows,
Who needs a map to cross this sea?
I've got my wit; it's good company.

Unraveling the Fabric of Now

Threads of chaos weave through my mind,
Patterns of laughter, so hard to find,
Tangled moments make a quilt of glee,
Each stitch is a shrug; it's all meant to be.

I trip on whims, like shoes untied,
With every misstep, I take in stride,
The fabric of time, a playful jest,
I'll wear my mismatched socks with zest.

Joyful Interludes in a Dreamless Night

Stars blink outside, they seem bemused,
The moon's a grin; the night's confused,
I count my giggles, not sheep tonight,
As they march in line, all dressed in white.

The clock ticks on, does it really care?
I sip my tea, and spin in the air,
Each moment's a dance, a silly fright,
I'm the queen of this dreamless night.

Finding Beauty in the Mundane

A spoon sings softly in my cup,
While toast croons loudly as I sup,
My dishes tumble in a playful spree,
Their clatter is music; it's wild and free.

Beneath the sun, I trip on grass,
Each blade a tickle; I'll let them pass,
In every wrinkle of my routine,
Lies a quirky joke, bright and keen.

Finding Solace in the Silence

In the whispers of the dark, I find my cheer,
A umpteenth pizza slice, my only dear.
The cat's judgmental gaze, I often flee,
Who needs a compass? I've got Netflix to see.

The goldfish swims in circles, looking perplexed,
I ponder my life choices, all so vexed.
Do socks really match? Is this even a quest?
Finding my purpose in a well-timed jest.

Emotions Adrift in an Open Sea

My boat is filled with snacks, as waves start to crash,
A bag of chips my anchor, in this whirlpool of trash.
The seagulls caw a tune, mocking my snack,
As I sail through this chaos, there's no turning back.

The ocean's a stage, where my worries play,
A dolphin jumps, probably judging my way.
I wave back dramatically, just being myself,
In this quirky sitcom, I'm the star on the shelf.

The Fragile Dance of Existence

I trip on my thoughts like a clumsy ballet,
Twirl with my coffee, kick worries away.
The floor is my friend, or a partner, I see,
In this dance of the absurd—just my soul and me.

The music is silent, but I hear my feet,
A symphony played by my heart's funky beat.
So I pirouette through chaos, a sight to behold,
Life's just a jester, with its antics so bold.

Awakenings Beneath an Empty Sky

The sky's just a canvas, with clouds in disarray,
Like my thoughts in the morning, they've gone out to play.
A bird tweets a joke, or so I assume,
And I laugh at the sun, as it lights up my room.

I sip on my coffee, while the day sneezes bright,
Rolling out of bed is my daily fright.
Yet, here I am grinning, with a cereal smile,
Just embracing the madness, for a little while.

Threads of an Unwoven Tapestry

Fuzzy threads hang without a clue,
They dance and twist, oh what a view!
Colors clash, a vibrant mess,
Yet here I am, in my own dress.

Lost my needle, forgot my plan,
Stitching dreams with a simple tan.
Who needs a map in this great mess?
I'll wear my laughter like a dress.

Laughter in the Emptiness

In a void that sings a silent song,
I cracked a joke, felt bold, not wrong.
The echoes chuckled, made me grin,
Seriouser thoughts? They couldn't win.

Balloons floated in the empty space,
I snorted once, outran the chase.
With nothing but ghosts to cheer me on,
I danced around till the break of dawn.

Searching for Splinters of Light

In shadows thick, I peek and pry,
Hoping to find a slice of sky.
A beam! A glimmer, oh so bright,
I laugh, trip over my own delight.

Scanning the floor for crumbs of cheer,
A shattered glass might just endear.
I throw my hands and spin around,
In this silly hunt, joy is found.

Stillness Amidst the Chaos

Amidst the whirl, I sit and sip,
A coffee cup, my captain's ship.
Chaos twirls, a wild ballet,
I sip and smile, come what may.

Juggling life like it's a game,
Each drop and spill, I feel the same.
In every mess, a chuckle lives,
And in the scramble, chaos gives.

Sipping from an Empty Cup

I sit with my mug, it's quite a show,
Its promises empty, like a glass for a woe.
I joke with a crumb from yesterday's toast,
In a circus of chaos, I'm the punchline the most.

A sip of nothing, it warms my hand,
As I ponder the jokes no one planned.
Why search for a purpose in a tepid brew?
When laughter's the answer, it's steeped in the skew.

The coffee grounds whisper, "Don't take it too hard!"
My hopes are like foam, they've just been jarred.
I nod at my cup, give a smile, a wink,
And toast to confusion — I'm not on the brink.

So here's to the nothing, the humor, the jest,
A life full of giggles can't be all that less.
My mug's always empty, but laughter's the fill,
In this game of absurd, I'm free of the chill.

Unraveling Threads of Purpose

I knitted a scarf with intentions so grand,
But ended up tangled, can't understand.
Each loop is a ponder, each stitch an embrace,
I've made quite a mess, but I laugh in the space.

The yarn that unraveled, what joy it did bring,
As I looked for a reason, the needles took wing.
A colorful chaos, a fashion faux pas,
But who needs a motive when you've got a caw?

I wear my threads wildly, a slapstick delight,
With patterns that twirl through the day and the night.
As I dance in this fabric of whimsy and cheer,
I laugh with each twist, without much of a steer.

So here's to the threads that make no sense at all,
To the fun in the futile, let's have a ball!
In this tapestry woven with moments of glee,
I find joy in the knot, a life wild and free.

A Journey Without a Destination

With a suitcase of dreams and a map full of holes,
I traveled the world, not chasing my goals.
Each step was a stumble, a giggle, a fall,
In pursuit of the nonsense, I found it in sprawl.

The roads led to nowhere, a path to delight,
Where punchlines and paths gleamed under moonlight.
A compass that spins just won't settle my fate,
But who needs direction when I have a plate?

I feasted on laughter and danced with a bee,
Each detour a jest, brilliant as can be.
Oh, glory in chaos, my itinerary laughs,
With a wink from the universe in all of its gaffs.

So, here's to the wanderers lost in their cheer,
Who find joy in the journey, with nothing to clear.
In this spectacle, silly, my heart takes to flight,
And I revel in the whimsy, embracing the light.

Shadows of a Fleeting Dream

In the corner of dreams, where shadows do play,
A thought tumbles down, in an amusing ballet.
It hops like a rabbit, it twirls like a clown,
Leaving giggles behind as it flops upside down.

Peeking through curtains of whimsical thought,
I chase after wisps of the moments I've sought.
Each shadow's a whisper, a tickle, a jest,
Caressing my troubles, it's really the best.

So here I am laughing, a fool in disguise,
With a pocket of humor and stars in my eyes.
If dreams are but shadows, for real they are bright,
And absurdity dances in the absence of night.

I'll twirl with the phantoms of giggles and glee,
For in this brief motion, I'm simply just me.
Embracing the fleeting, I find my way through,
In shadows of liveliness, I've nothing to rue.

Embracing the Absurd

I wear mismatched socks for fun,
A fashion statement, just begun.
Chasing shadows in the sun,
Laughter echoes, we've already won.

The cat thinks he's the king of all,
While I trip over pillows, I might fall.
We dance to tunes of a distant call,
In a world so weird, we have a ball.

The clock ticks slowly inside my head,
Counting the jellybeans I've fed.
Life's a farce, who needs a thread?
I'll wear my crown of thoughts instead!

Juggling dreams like they're old laundry,
Pretending life's a big ol' party.
Who needs a plan? Not even Tony,
Here's to the silly, let's get gnarly!

Constellations Without Destiny

Stars are just holes in the sky,
Each twinkle a wink from those up high.
Their destination? Up for a try,
And I'll keep guessing as I lie.

A toaster talks to my favorite spoon,
Imagining dances under the moon.
Together we sing a joyful tune,
While the fridge hums a funky cartoon.

Maps are doodles on paper sheets,
Leading me to my fridge, oh what treats!
Adventure awaits in small feats,
As I shuffle, with mismatched beats.

Sailing on thoughts as boats of cheese,
There's magic in the simple breeze.
Life's wild moments, just like these,
Make all the sense—if you please!

Echoes of Existence

I talk to my plants, they never reply,
They listen well, no need to be shy.
In their silence, my thoughts fly high,
They nod along; they're kind of sly.

Walking in circles, I keep the score,
Counting my steps, then losing more.
The ducks all quack, a loud uproar,
As I ponder life's cheeky folklore.

Finding meaning in absurdity,
Wearing my cereal for a hat, you see.
Skits in head, that's my decree,
Live it out loud, carefree esprit!

Each day's a game with quirky rules,
Hiding from adults, those serious fools.
Playtime's the key; joy is the jewels,
In this big playground, we're all just tools!

The Art of Being Lost

I wander streets with no clear goal,
Each twist and turn feeds the soul.
Lost in thought, I found my role,
A mere jester, live for the whole.

Maps are suggestions; I just laugh,
Recalculating paths, but on my behalf.
With every step, I craft my gaffe,
Life's a riddle, and I'm the chaff.

The squirrels hold council, plotting schemes,
While I sip my coffee, lost in dreams.
Together we scheme, or so it seems,
In this circus life, where laughter beams.

So here's to crazy, forking roads,
Embracing chaos, offloads and goads.
Waving at dogs, and stealing codes,
In the art of losing, my spirit explodes!

Crafting Hope from Shadows

In a world of cheese and dreams,
I dance with wobbly knees.
With ice cream dripping down my face,
I chase my giggles, time won't erase.

I'm juggling life with rubber chickens,
Chasing joy in all its quicken.
Each mishap a funny little tune,
I'm here to laugh beneath the moon.

With sock puppets and silly hats,
I'll sway with cats and wear the sprats.
If meaning's lost, I'll thrift some fun,
Let's wrestle with the setting sun.

So raise a toast with fizzy pops,
To bouncing hopes and funny flops.
In shadows deep, we'll find our spark,
Crafting laughter in the dark.

Voices of the Unheard

In a crowded room, I'm quite the ghost,
With whispers loud, but actions boast.
Shouting to the plants, my only fans,
They nod in silence, forming bands.

I converse with socks; they share their woes,
And argue if they match the clothes.
The fridge hums tunes of forgotten meals,
While laughter dances upon our heels.

Echoes of jokes float in the air,
Invisible cheers, we quibble and dare.
We're all a circus, in geeky grace,
Swinging to rhythms our hearts embrace.

So let's be loud in the quiet places,
Painting the world with silly faces.
For in our voices, though seldom heard,
We'll craft a song without a word.

Fleeting Whispers of Existence

Life's a hiccup, a sneeze, a laugh,
Like a rollercoaster drawn on a half.
I chase the wind on wobbly wheels,
As time slips by, I spin with squeals.

With every hiccup, I'll try to soar,
And hide my fumbles by the door.
I've wrapped my dreams in bubble wrap,
To pop them softly in a nap.

Tickling butterflies with a silly song,
I twirl in circles, where I belong.
Life's a jester in a tangled jest,
I'm here for the laugh, forget the rest.

So I'll dance with shadows, sing with glee,
And pretend that I've got it all figured—me.
With fleeting whispers, we'll make a sound,
In the chaos of fun, joy will abound.

Embracing the Void

In a void where logic looks away,
I juggle ducks, come what may.
With each quack, I crack a smile,
Finding joy in the absurdity of the mile.

I wear mismatched socks and fear the fall,
In this grand puzzle, we trip and sprawl.
I embrace the awkward, the clumsy dance,
Where silence lingers, I take a chance.

With lemons tossed, we make our cheer,
Wishing for meaning, but never near.
So we sip on laughter, sweet and sour,
Prancing in moments, hour by hour.

Let's toast the empty, raise our glass,
For in this void, true friends amass.
In the silly, the chaos, we find the glow,
Embracing laughter, as we let it flow.

Resilience in the Face of Nothingness

Woke up today, tripped on my shoe,
Fell right into coffee, oh what a view.
The universe chuckles, but I laugh along,
With each little blunder, I sing my own song.

Jelly on bagels, a delicate crime,
I dance with the chaos, I'm wasting no time.
The fridge hums a tune, the cat gives a stare,
In this grand performance, I'm happily rare.

Clouds might be different, they wear silly hats,
I tell them my secrets, and they answer with chats.
Though questions keep swirling like socks in the wash,
I stumble through answers and give life a squash.

So bring on the nonsense, the weird, and the wild,
For every strange moment, a giggle's compiled.
And if all of it crumbles, I'll still find a way,
A clown in this circus, I'm here to stay.

Dancing in the Shadows of Doubt

Tiptoe through worries, I'm no ballet star,
Yet dancing on questions, I'm always ajar.
The shadows, they whisper, 'You'll never be free,'
I twirl with my doubts, sipping sweet cups of tea.

A hat made of troubles sits crooked on me,
But I wear it with style, like a grand jubilee.
If life throws a curve, I'll juggle my fears,
With a grin that says, 'Bring me the tears!'

The moon winks at me, what a peculiar sight,
As I trip over dreams, but I'm feeling all right.
With a sprinkle of madness, I shimmy and sway,
In the dance of uncertainty, I'll find my own way.

So here's to the laughter, the odd and the rare,
To finding the joy in the things we don't share.
For in every dark corner, I'll twist and I'll glide,
A playful little dancer, with humor as my guide.

Starry Skies Above an Empty Heart

Under the blanket of void, I lay low,
Counting my feelings, like stars in a show.
For every dead end, I'll plant a bouquet,
Of quirky reflections that brighten my day.

A heart full of giggles, with room for a laugh,
I build my own castle, complete with a staff.
With stardust for glitter, I'm dressed to impress,
In the emptiness, I find my own mess.

The cosmic joke's on me, I'm the punchline anew,
But I wear it with pride, like a well-suited shoe.
For every star's twinkle, there's nonsense to share,
In the vastness of nothing, I'm still standing there.

So I toast to the void, let it serve me some cheer,
For even in silence, I know I am here.
A comet of laughter, a wink in the dark,
And in my wild universe, I'll always leave a mark.

Beneath the Weight of Silence

Silence is heavy, like too much cake,
I wobble and giggle, oh what a mistake.
In the quietest moments, I chat with my thoughts,
They murmur back softly, tying up knots.

With pillows for company, I preach to the wall,
About how the sky seems to have lost its call.
Though echoes of nothing, they come back in style,
I shrug with a grin, and I pause for a while.

Beneath all the weight, I float like a clown,
With laughter as currency, I'll never drown.
For every wild whisper that beckons my name,
I'll dance in the shadows, embracing the game.

So here's to the silence, let it follow me near,
For in all its softness, I find my frontier.
With a chuckle at nothing, I'll conquer each sigh,
In the grand hush of life, I'll always fly high.

When Tomorrow is Just a Whisper

The clock ticks loud, but I just snooze,
My dreams argue over the latest news.
Cereal with a hint of yesterday's fate,
Laughing at the future while I contemplate.

A plan to jog, I make it in my head,
But Netflix calls and I stay in bed.
I dance with shadows in my living room,
Who needs a purpose when I've got this tune?

Each cup of coffee, a philosophical quest,
With sugar and cream, I know I'm blessed.
The cat judges me for the third slice of pie,
Life's absurdities can always make me sigh.

So here I sit with my book of old jokes,
Finding clarity in these foolish pokes.
Life may not be a neatly tied bow,
But laughter's my anchor, it's all I know.

Lost Letters in an Unread Book

A book on the shelf whispers tales untold,
Tales of heroes, braver and bold.
I flip through pages, still stuck on the first,
Guess I'll leave them waiting, they'll just have to burst.

Ink stains and dust make for a fine retreat,
With letters that mingle, oh, where are my feet?
A character sips tea, lost in a plot,
I ponder existence, then forget what I thought.

The bookmarks are shouting, 'Pick us, we're fun!'
Instead, I choose naps under the warm sun.
The words tease my mind, but I'm not quite prepared,
To turn all their stories, they'd leave me ensnared.

As each letter waits for its breath to be taken,
I chuckle away, feeling quite unshaken.
Maybe one day, I'll dive in and read,
But until then, blissful ignorance is my creed.

Embracing the Fractured Self

Mirror, mirror, who's the best of the bunch?
Oh wait, that's just me in a munchy lunch.
Wearing my quirks like a badge on display,
I'd trade all my wisdom for humor today.

My flaws gather 'round like a merry parade,
Each one with a story, a joke well played.
A heart that's mosaic, bursting with cheer,
I stumble through life, but that's just my gear.

My socks don't match, but my spirit's on fire,
In the chaos of self, I find my desire.
Flawed like a painting with strokes gone awry,
My laughter's the glue that keeps me nearby.

So let the world dance on this jumbled path,
With hiccups and giggles, I'll find my own math.
In the puzzle of me, I relish the strife,
Who knew broken pieces could laugh at life?

Where Breaths Meet Endless Possibilities

Breath in, breath out, like a quirky old tune,
Life's a circus act beneath the bright moon.
A juggler of hopes, I fumble and cheer,
As two left feet try to find their way here.

Each inhale's a chance, each exhale a joke,
Taking my stumbles, not just a poke.
I whirl like a dervish on this crooked street,
Life throws confetti with every heart beat.

The clouds gather up with their thoughts on display,
They rain down wisdom in a jumbled bouquet.
And I'm caught in the storm, yet I'm dancing anew,
Finding the punchline in all that I do.

With a wink and a grin, life's a comedy show,
And I'm the headliner, in case you didn't know.
So let's raise a glass to the wild and the free,
For each breath we take is a chance to just be.

Fragments of a Dream Yet to be

In the fridge I found a cheese,
A beacon in my midnight freeze.
It hummed a tune, a cheesy fling,
In a world that's void of anything.

I tripped on socks while chasing light,
Clumsy feet on a Tuesday night.
Thought I could dance, but I just fell,
Life's a joke, can't you tell?

Bananas on the kitchen shelf,
Whisper secrets to themselves.
They peel away the mundane fear,
As laughter echoes loud and clear.

A cat stares blankly from the chair,
Judging life without a care.
I wave and shrug in sweet defeat,
He's the king, my humble seat.

Ephemeral Joys in a Constant Wind

A paper boat sails down the stream,
   Its captain lost in a daydream.
Tick-tock goes the clock's old face,
  Time flies by, but leaves no trace.

I danced with shadows on the wall,
  And stumbled back into the hall.
With each misstep, I took a chance,
    Life's a laugh, a silly dance.

Cereal for dinner? Why not, I say!
Marshmallows cheer me on all day.
As laughter bubbles from the bowl,
Who knew chaos could be so whole?

A squirrel stole my sandwich out,
  With acorns singing all about.
In this wild, unpredictable spree,
    Nature's joke is on me!

The Essence of Being Uncertain

A thought just crossed my cloudy mind,
Was it a gem or just unkind?
The lightbulb flickers, sparks a fray,
In this circus, I'll just play.

Palm trees wobble in a breeze,
Their leaves are flapping, quite a tease.
I stand perplexed, don't take a seat,
As life does waltz, so light on feet.

My cat insists on lordship's reign,
While I maintain a cloak of pain.
Yet giggles sprout like daisies do,
In chaos blooms a joy that's true.

The catnip's here, let's ponder fate,
When all I want is just a plate.
Tomorrow's code remains unclear,
But in laughter, I'll persevere.

A Tapestry of Question Marks

A knitted scarf hangs lopsided,
Each loop a question I decided.
What's the meaning? Who can say?
I wear it proudly every day.

The toaster pops, it's such a scene,
Is breakfast made for kings or queens?
Burnt edges whisper tales of fate,
As butter melts, it's never late.

In a world of 'what ifs', I shove,
Each whim a flight — or was it love?
I spin around in this grand quest,
While socks unite, forgotten vest.

A dog named Frank just stole my shoe,
He prances off, quite proud and new.
We chase this whimsy, a silly spark,
For in this life, we leave our mark.

Capturing Time's Elusive Dance

In a world of mixed up clocks,
Tick-tock often meets paradox.
I chase the hours with silly glee,
While time just giggles, oh so free.

I try to catch a minute loose,
It darts away, it's quite profuse.
Like trying to juggle jellybeans,
Or walking dogs in roller skates sheens.

Each second slips like buttered toast,
I toast to moments I love the most.
With every laugh, I twist and twirl,
In this absurd and wacky whirl.

So let's embrace this laughing race,
With quirky steps, I find my place.
If time won't stop for me, that's fine,
I'll dance around it with some wine!

Navigating Through Broken Compass

With compass spinning like a top,
I wander round, I'll never stop.
The North is lost, the South is shy,
But hey, at least the snacks are nigh!

Maps are just a jigsaw game,
I'm lost, but never feel the shame.
Every turn just leads to fun,
A treasure hunt, my life's a pun.

I trip on dreams like chunky shoes,
In this maze, I can't refuse.
A wrong turn, I spot a rainbow,
And take a leap, just to see where I go.

With every misstep, I smile wide,
Adventures bloom, I take in stride.
The stars are shining out of tune,
But I'll groove to my own wayward tune!

Between Dreams and Dusk

Between the dreams and fading light,
I play peek-a-boo with the night.
Moonbeams gossip, shadows chuckle,
As reality gives a playful buckle.

I hug my pillows, oh so tight,
Chasing fables, taking flight.
In this realm where silliness reigns,
I slip through cracks like sugar canes.

The dusk hums tunes from a far-off place,
A melody wears a goofy face.
With every yawn, I tap dance slow,
In a world where giggles overflow.

So here I am, a dreamer bold,
In twilight's arms, a joy to hold.
With laughter echoing through the night,
I waltz between the wrong and right!

Holding Tight to Fleeting Instants

I grasp at moments like a prize,
Like bubbles floating to the skies.
Each one pops, a peal of laughter,
As I chase shadows, ever after.

Silly memories a tangled thread,
Tickle my mind like a feather bed.
I stumble, tumble, fall in glee,
Bounding through time, wild and free.

Moments flutter like penny-birds,
Each one sings without any words.
A giggle here, a snort over there,
I gather laughter without a care.

So hold tight to what makes you grin,
In every chaos, let fun begin.
With fleeting instants, life's a spree,
I dance through time, just wait and see!

The Color of Uncertainty

In a sea of gray, I paint my days,
With splashes of red and odd purple rays.
A dance of doubt with a hint of glee,
I trip on my thoughts, quite merrily.

The sun laughs down, then hides away,
While I juggle dreams like a child's play.
A canvas of moments — all out of whack,
But who needs a plan? I'll wing the track.

I wear mismatched socks and a crooked grin,
While pondering where this wild ride begins.
Each step I take feels a bit absurd,
But oh, what a tale if you've ever heard!

So here I stand, in the midst of my jest,
With a heart like a balloon, floating at best.
If life's a puzzle, I'm missing a piece,
But laughter's my guide, at least that won't cease.

Struggling with the Silence

In a crowded room of empty chairs,
I attempt small talk with lingering stares.
My jokes fall flat like pancakes unturned,
While silence around me burns and churns.

I stutter and stumble, my words take flight,
Like clumsy little birds lost in the night.
I giggle nervously; it's quite a sight,
As silence gives me a comedic fright.

The clock ticks loud, it mocks my state,
As I search for a friend who won't hesitate.
But laughter is fleeting, it dances away,
Leaving me chuckling like a child at play.

So I'll raise a toast to this awkward show,
To silence, my friend, and the comedy flow.
In this quirky world where we all coexist,
I find the punchline in each little twist.

In the Lull Between Questions

Questions swirl like leaves in the breeze,
While I sit back, munching on cheese.
Why are we here? What's the grand plan?
I giggle and wonder, where's my soda can?

Between 'what' and 'how', I lose my way,
Laughing at thoughts that simply won't stay.
Am I a hamster, stuck in a wheel?
I chuckle aloud, it's all part of the deal.

My mind drifts on, a balloon set free,
Floating through life like a bumblebee.
Questions pop up; I let out a snort,
A circus of chaos, my favorite sport.

So when the next query comes knocking near,
I'll hide my confusion behind laughter and cheer.
In the lull where we ponder, I sip my brew,
And forget all those answers I never knew.

Fables of Forgotten Intent

Once upon a time, in a land of maybe,
Lived a cat with dreams of being all shady.
He plotted and schemed to catch a grand mouse,
But never quite managed, just lounged in his house.

A wise old owl perched high in a tree,
Said, "Life's just a joke — don't take it too seriously!"
The cat rolled his eyes and sipped on some cream,
As the owl cawed loudly, "Don't follow that dream!"

Later one night, with a flick of his tail,
The cat pondered deep over a half-eaten snail.
"Fables of hope or just stories of woe?
Perhaps I'll skip chasing, just enjoy the show."

After all my friend, isn't humor the thread?
In tales of the lost, we find what we dread.
So here goes the cat, with a chuckle and grin,
To bask in the laughter where madness begins.

The Canvas of Unsketched Beginnings

A blank page lies in front of me,
With crayons sharp and ready to be.
I draw a cat that looks like cheese,
And wonder if it's art, if it's a tease.

The world spins madly, like a dreidel,
While I write a novel with no title.
My coffee spills, my muse takes flight,
But hey, at least my socks are bright.

I paint my dreams with colors bold,
Like a story half-told, never old.
Each brushstroke whispers, "Hey, relax!"
While I dodge my life's little cracks.

In this wild art class we call our fate,
I ponder if there's a real escape.
But laughter creeps in, like a best friend,
Who tickles your brain till the worries end.

Witness to a Fleeting Moment

I stood in line for coffee one fine morn,
Caught sight of a squirrel, feeling reborn.
It danced like it owned the whole block,
While I pondered if my hair was a shock.

The barista sneezed, it flew like a dove,
And suddenly, I questioned life and love.
Does this caffeine hold the universe's key?
Or just a sugar rush and a little glee?

Moments flit past, like fireflies in June,
Bright flashes of joy, like a silly tune.
I balance on thoughts, like a clown on a wire,
With dreams that ignite but never conspire.

In the chaos of life, I trip and I fall,
But I laugh, here I am, and I'm having a ball.
As reality spins like a carnival ride,
I hang on tight, with a goofy pride.

Stories Beneath the Stars

Stars twinkle like they've had too much wine,
Each one a story, a joke, a line.
I ask them my dreams, they giggle and twirl,
As I contemplate if I'm missing a pearl.

The moon, my companion, a grumpy old chap,
Whispers advice like it's taking a nap.
I tell him of plans and he yawns with a grin,
"Have you considered just diving in?"

Galaxies spin in a cosmic ballet,
While I search for meaning, come what may.
But each wish I cast feels like a shower,
Of thousand glittery confetti, a little power.

So here under skies painted black and gold,
I chuckle at life, as the stars unfold.
For laughter's a treasure, a guide in disguise,
That makes sense of the madness under these skies.

Mosaic of Silenced Thoughts

In the silence, thoughts take flight,
Like balloons at a fair, colorful and light.
One pops and shrieks, the crowd starts to cheer,
Am I hosting a circus? Oh dear, oh dear!

I build a mosaic with broken dreams,
Pasting them down with tape and beams.
Each piece a giggle, a whisper of fate,
As I craft my life, yes, it's never too late.

The quiet hums like a fridge at night,
And my heart's a drum with a silly delight.
I dance with the doubts, a pirouette glance,
While I search for a reason, or just take a chance.

In this zany puzzle, I stitch and I sew,
Each laugh adds color, each giggle a glow.
Because in the end, as my fabric unfolds,
It's the joy in the chaos that never grows old.

Nurturing the Unknowable

In a world of questions galore,
I'd drown in thoughts, but I swim ashore.
Chasing tails like a cat on a spree,
Whispers of wisdom, you won't hear from me.

Juggling socks that never match,
Finding sense in a pickle, a scratch.
The fridge hums secrets, or maybe it's me,
Twirls of confusion, a waltz of the free.

Laughter bubbles like a pot on the stove,
Stirring deep while we pretend to be rove.
Chasing squirrels in the park of the mind,
Crafting nonsense that most would call unrefined.

Yet here I stand with a grin on my face,
Dancing with shadows in an enigmatic place.
Life's a circus with me in the ring,
Clowning around, that's my kind of fling.

Hearts Beating in Monochrome

To paint my days in colors so bright,
But all I find is shades of night.
Dancing on rain clouds, or so I believe,
Sometimes I chuckle, sometimes I grieve.

Pondering life like a loaf of stale bread,
Smirking at thoughts that dance in my head.
Maybe wisdom's a hat I can't wear,
Yet I'll strut like a peacock without a care.

In a black and white world, I juggle some gray,
Witty remarks are the games that I play.
Digging for treasures in mundane affairs,
I find a gold coin, just hidden downstairs.

So here's to the quirks in the rhythm of fate,
With a laugh and a wink, I seal my own fate.
To dance through this life with a skip and a hop,
For deep in the silence, I know I won't stop.

The Search for Meaning in the Mundane

Cereal for breakfast, a mystical quest,
Finding deep answers in crumbs of the best.
Spilling my coffee as I ponder the deep,
Life's riddles hiding where reminders sleep.

Remote controls are the keys to my fate,
Channel surfing to find something great.
With socks on my hands, I dance in delight,
Searching for magic in the dim morning light.

The clock ticks louder than my racing heart,
Each tick, a reminder, a whimsical art.
Life's puzzle is missing a piece or two,
But I'll fit a rubber band and call it my glue.

So raise a glass to the trivial things,
To the joy in the chaos that insanity brings.
In moments of silence, I puff out my chest,
With laughter in tow, I feel truly blessed.

Grounded Yet Floating

I'm anchored to earth but my mind's in the clouds,
Floating on whims, as I'm lost in the crowds.
With spaghetti for thoughts and meatballs for plans,
I navigate life with the grace of a dance.

Raindrops like confetti fall soft on my skin,
As I twirl and I jive, let the madness begin.
Living on bread crumbs from yesterday's meal,
Hoping some wisdom might suddenly reveal.

Every sunrise, a brand-new surprise,
I fumble and tumble as the day starts to rise.
The grass beneath tickles my toes, oh so bright,
Chasing my worries like butterflies in flight.

So here I stand, a marvel of grace,
A jester in life's unpredictable race.
With laughter as my compass, I wander and roam,
Grounded yet floating, I'm finding my home.

Threads of Laughter in a Silent Room

In a room where silence bides,
I laugh at shadows, sneaky strides.
The walls are bare, but jokes abound,
Echoing giggles, a comic sound.

The clock just ticks, no ticks or tocks,
I wear mismatched socks, like crazy socks.
Clocks have no sense of time, you see,
Especially when they're late just like me.

The chair's my friend, it creaks and groans,
It tells me tales of silly tones.
With every grin, the light grows bright,
Even in darkness, I find delight.

So bring your jokes and silly puns,
And let's pretend we're all just once.
In this quiet room, laughter blooms,
Filling the air with joy that zooms.

Love Letters to the Unknown

I penned a letter to the void,
My thoughts in ink, a heart deployed.
With scribbled lines, I flirt with fate,
Each phrase a dare, my soul's first date.

Dear mystery, how are you today?
I sent my worries far away.
With rubber stamps and silly seals,
Your name in rhymes is how it feels.

I wrapped my hopes in silly string,
Tied them up tight for you to bring.
My dreams may waltz on paper planes,
Giggles await where sunshine rains.

Oh, unknown love, you're quite the tease,
Yet in your chaos, I find my ease.
I'll write you letters, one by one,
In the end, maybe we'll have fun.

Wandering Through Curious Landscapes

I wander through fields of odd-shaped rocks,
Where logic ends and silliness mocks.
Trees wear hats and lakes sip tea,
Adventure awaits, come dance with me.

The path is built of gummy bears,
With chocolate rivers, no worldly cares.
Every step, a gummy crinkle sound,
In this odd world, joy is found.

Mountains laugh, they tickle the sky,
Clouds roll in, they wink and sigh.
The sun is a jester, bright and bold,
In these landscapes, the heart won't grow old.

So join my quest for quirky sights,
Let's gather up the day and nights.
Amidst the strange, we'll build a stage,
And laugh through life, page by page.

Flickers of Hope in Darkened Days

When shadows fall, I wiggle my toes,
Each step a dance, wherever it goes.
Lemonade stands grow in the gloom,
With laughter served in every room.

The clouds may pout, but I won't fret,
With silly hats and my best pet.
In drizzles of doubt, I'll jump and play,
Splashing puddles, come what may.

The stars are shy, they hide away,
But I'll toss wishes like a bouquet.
With each heartbeat, I'll light a spark,
Chasing whispers in the dark.

So when the nights seem cold and bleak,
Just wink at life, and take a peek.
In the winks of joy, I find my way,
A flickering candle to light the day.

Whispers in the Void

In a world of jumbled thoughts,
I chase my socks, lost in the fog.
The fridge hums a secret tune,
While I ponder the dance of a dog.

Cereal dreams upon my plate,
Milk splashes like a wild parade.
I laugh at the cat chasing its tail,
While I search for my keys, I'm delayed.

Nothing makes sense, it's quite absurd,
But here I stand, no need for a word.
I tickle the universe's fancy,
And make friends with thoughts that are blurred.

So let's toast to the chaos and mess,
With a wink and a dance, I confess.
Not every quest needs a grand end,
Sometimes laughter's the cure for distress.

Dancing with Uncertainty

I twirl on the edge of my bed,
Wondering if breakfast is worth the dread.
With a sock on my foot, I try to prance,
But my roommate is judging my dance.

The alarm clock yells, but I'm still in dreams,
Finding answers in toast's golden creams.
The toaster pops; it yells, 'surprise!',
As I slip in my shoes with mismatched ties.

Who says I must know where I'm going?
The spaghetti of life keeps its flowing.
I giggle at fate as it trips on a cone,
And call it my partner, not alone.

So give me the silly, the weird, the fun,
In the dance of the absurd, we've only begun.
With laughter my guide and joy in the lead,
Let's swirl through the chaos like the wind in a seed.

The Weight of Wondering

With questions piled high on my plate,
I juggle my thoughts, a confusing fate.
Why do we ponder the why and the how,
While dogs bark loudly at shadows that bow?

The scale says I'm heavy, but maybe it's lies,
It could just be all of my unsaid goodbyes.
As the fridge hums its tune of regret,
I nod to the universe, not living in debt.

What if today brings a pie from the sky?
Can I order one please? I'll give it a try!
A sprinkle of laugh on the crust, so divine,
I'll savor the sweet, and dance in the brine.

So let's toss our worries like confetti in air,
For what's life without laughter, a bit of a flair?
With whimsy and chuckles and a grand sense of cheer,
Who needs clearer answers? I'm happy right here.

Shadows of a Silent Tomorrow

In the glow of the fridge, I ponder my fate,
As shadows of past snacks congregate.
I laugh at the milk, so expired, yet spry,
A time-traveling beverage; oh my, oh my!

Tomorrow stands still, like a turtle in shoes,
While I sip on coffee, confused with the blues.
The cat eyes me sideways, a judge in my plan,
As I trip on my thoughts like a one-legged man.

Who knew that the couch held secrets so deep?
It tells tales of napping while I count sheep.
In crannies and corners, I hide my delight,
With snacks in my pockets, I'm ready to fight.

So let's greet the day with a chuckle and grin,
With messy hair styles where chaos begins.
In the shadows of silence, I find out what's true,
Life's a joke, but I'm loving the view!

Echoes of Uncertainty

In a world that's upside down,
Clowns wear frowns, and kings wear crowns.
I lose my socks and find lost keys,
Bouncing through life like a bumblebee.

Thoughts like bubbles, they float and pop,
I trip on life and then I hop.
Chasing answers that run away,
Waltzing with chaos, what a display!

Laughter echoes in the night,
While shadows dance and take their flight.
I chuckle at the cosmic jest,
For each perplexity, there's room for rest.

So raise a glass to the absurd,
To the confusion that goes unheard.
We're all just players in this show,
With scripts that change, and winds that blow.

Finding Beauty in the Chaos

A cat in a box, or is it a plane?
The universe giggles, it's all the same.
I trip over my thoughts and my feet,
Life's a circus, not one to delete.

Painting rainbows with a mop,
While squirrels debate if they should stop.
The jester grins, but who carries on?
In this wild dance, what's so wrong?

Folding laundry while chasing dreams,
The toaster pops, and the cat screams.
In a world that's spinning like a top,
Finding joy in the chaos is the stop.

So here's to the hiccups, the slips, the falls,
To punctured plans and broken calls.
In the blend of colors, I find my hue,
Laughing at the mess, as if it's new.

The Art of Living Amidst Ambiguity

A penguin in a tux, but where's the dance?
Life's a taco, but missing the chance.
With each new riddle, I don my hat,
And wander the maze with my curious cat.

Juggling wishes like ripe tomatoes,
While dancing to tunes of overblown avocados.
The world's a puzzle with pieces misplaced,
Yet I treat every mess like a dessert to taste.

So I walk on the edge, a balance of laughs,
With clouds of confusion splitting in halves.
The doughnut shop's open, the latte's hot,
Embracing the chaos, it's all that I've got.

In a swirl of confetti, I take a leap,
For simplicity hides in the depths of the steep.
With a wink and a shrug, I'll sway through the gray,
In this circus of life, I'm here to stay.

Footprints on an Illusory Path

On paths of marshmallows, I strut and stutter,
Chasing my shadow while licking some butter.
Each footstep's pudding, each thought a mix,
Building a story of wobbly tricks.

I find my way through spaghetti strands,
Where logic disappears like castles of sand.
The stars are puzzled, and so am I,
Drifting like balloons in a blueberry sky.

With a sprinkle of giggles and a dash of grace,
I juggle my heart in this whimsical space.
Each wiggle, each wobble, a brand new chart,
Skimming the edges of poetry and art.

So here's to the footprints on roads unclear,
To the laughter that echoes when chaos draws near.
For in every sigh, and every little laugh,
I sketch my own map, finding joy in the path.

Holding Hands with the Abyss

I tripped on my own thoughts today,
Fell straight into a dark ballet.
The abyss offered me a snack,
I said, "Thanks, but I've got a back!"

I danced with shadows, can't you see?
They took me out for a cup of tea.
We laughed about the empty space,
Turns out, it's just a chilling place!

A ghost joked, 'It's pretty nice here,'
I replied, 'I'm just grabbing a beer.'
Instead of angst, we toasted fate,
To nothingness, our funny date!

In the void, I found a friend or two,
All wearing socks that didn't match, boo!
So if you ever feel a tug,
Just remember, it's all a shrug!

Searching for Light in the Unlit Corners

I searched for light in my own mess,
Found a sock, no need to stress!
It whispered tales of lost and found,
A comedy of laundry all around!

Under the couch, a dust bunny sighed,
Trying to be my friend, but I cried.
'Please don't go, I need company,'
It rolled away; how rude, don't you see?

The fridge hummed a tune of despair,
Leftovers sang, 'We're still here, don't care!'
I danced with expired dairy cheese,
Feeling like royalty, if you please!

In the corners where shadows creep,
I found a laughter that was deep.
Life's a riddle; it doesn't care,
Just giggle loudly and comb your hair!

The Paradox of Breathing

I woke up this morning, took a breath,
Wondered if it might lead to death.
But then I sneezed and felt alive,
Paradox, it seems, can help us thrive!

Inhale the chaos, exhale the calm,
Life's a wild ride—the ultimate balm.
Laughter fizzes like soda pop,
I hiccuped twice; oh, I'll never stop!

I'm here with hiccups and wild dreams,
Dancing in the sunlit beams.
Each breath a joke; each sigh a laugh,
The universe's weird autograph!

So if you feel things don't quite fit,
Just take a breath and make a wit.
In the paradox, let's find our cheer,
With laughter that twinkles, oh so near!

An Ode to the Unseen

To the invisible beings all around,
I toast to you, in laughter we're bound.
You trip over chairs, and fall through walls,
I see your antics and hear your calls!

The ghosts in my closet crack a grin,
As I dance clumsily, joy within.
You'd think they'd help me find my socks,
But they're too busy placing pranks like clocks!

In shadows, you cheer me on today,
With swirling whispers, you make me sway.
To the unseen forces that play with fate,
Let's roll our eyes at the things we create!

So here's to laughter, both near and far,
In this wild journey, we are the stars.
We'll twirl in the night, all shadows and grace,
Finding joy in this nonsensical space!

The Heartbeat of the Aimless

I wake up in the morning, still in my bed,
The alarm just a suggestion, so I hit snooze instead.
Coffee in my hand, spilling all on the floor,
I laugh at the mess, life's a quirky chore.

The cat gives me side-eye, judging my ways,
I wonder if he knows it's just one of those days.
I search for my shoes, still lost in the fray,
Maybe I'll wear slippers, and call it okay.

Outside, the world dances, it's a clumsy waltz,
Each person a puzzle, with bright little faults.
I join in the chaos, ready or not,
Maybe I'm lost, but I like this spot.

With giggles and prances, we stumble and weave,
In a life without measures, what's hard to believe?
Each moment a riddle, yet laughter we find,
Just wandering aimlessly, it's fun to be blind.

Moments Captured in Time's Embrace

The clock on the wall is a stubborn old dude,
Ticking away while I dance in my mood.
Snapshots of laughter, like butterflies caught,
Moments we treasure, though meaning is naught.

I trip over memories, they laugh as they fall,
Chasing the clock like it owes me a call.
In my mind's messy attic, I find little things,
A sock and a sandwich, oh what joy it brings!

The sunbeams are playful, they tickle my nose,
While I'm busy pondering where the time goes.
With pie in the sky, dreams float like air,
In this tangled-up game, I just do not care.

So here's to the moments that slip through my hands,
Wrapped up in distractions and faraway plans.
Each giggle and wiggle, a dance in the haze,
Embracing the nonsense, in whimsical ways.

The Poetry of Fleeting Hours

An hourglass tips, and the sand falls away,
I sit in my chair, making up my own play.
Each grain a reminder, a jest in disguise,
As I giggle at time with my wide-open eyes.

I write silly verses on napkins and dreams,
While reality teases and gives me the beams.
A jester in life, I laugh at the clock,
Time's just a prankster, a really bad rock.

In cafes and parks, I search for the knight,
Who's lost his shiny armor, and prefers to take flight.
Together we squabble, we dance in a stew,
These moments are fleeting, as I sip my brew.

So here's to the giggles and the nonsense I find,
A riddle unwritten, with laughter entwined.
For every tick-tock of this comedic show,
I'll savor each moment, wherever I go.

A Journey Without a Map

With no GPS signal, I drift and I roam,
Each street is a story, but I'm far from home.
The map is a myth, just a scrap in my hand,
As I wander through life, like a solo band.

I wear mismatched socks, just to upset the norm,
And serenade pigeons, my feathered form.
With every strange turn, I chuckle with glee,
For the journey is silly, yet joyful and free.

The people I meet, they're oddballs like me,
Swapping lost fortunes for cups of green tea.
We laugh at our plans that go sideways and spin,
Each wander's a story, and I'm grinning within.

So here's to the paths that lead nowhere at all,
Where the punchlines are waiting, just waiting for a call.
With every misstep, I embrace the unknown,
In this journey without maps, I truly feel at home.

Living on the Edge of Disbelief

I woke up today with a sock on my head,
My cat gave me judgment, as if I was dead.
The coffee was screaming, the toast seemed to sigh,
Even my plants whispered, "Just let it fly!"

I pondered the cosmos, the stars' silent cheer,
While my neighbor's dog barked, "What's the fuss here?"
I laughed at the chaos, embraced the absurd,
In a world that is wild, my thoughts felt unheard.

Pancakes on Tuesday, who made up that rule?
The fridge is my canvas, the kitchen my school.
A dance with the dishes, a waltz with the broom,
In the midst of this nonsense, I thrive in the gloom.

So let's toast to the moments we can't quite ignore,
With a glass full of pickle juice, who could ask for more?
Life's like a circus, I'm just part of the show,
As the ringmaster laughs, saying, "Here we go!"

Hummingbird Hearts and Empty Nest

There's a hummingbird buzzing, with nowhere to land,
My heart does a jig, it's as if it had planned.
The flowers are laughing, they know what I mean,
In a dance of the absurd, I'm caught in between.

An empty nest echoes, a place once so loud,
It's like a small bubble, lost in the crowd.
I chase after giggles, old memories flee,
But the cheese in the fridge has some facts to decree.

So let's toast to the sparrows, the wise and the old,
With tales of our follies, and laughter retold.
The world might be quirky, but I can't help but sing,
To the tune of our nonsense, together we swing.

There's joy in the chaos, in every strange sight,
With hummingbird hearts, we'll dance through the night.
Even when stillness is all that we get,
I'll chirp like a bird, without any regret.

A Breath of Air in an Endless Sea

The waves are a riddle, a dance on the shore,
I'm paddling hard, but I'm still wanting more.
A fish just winked at me, said, "What's the plan?"
I shrugged, did a backflip, said, "Just being a man!"

The sun keeps on smiling, while clouds play hardball,
I'm chasing my shadow, but it's having a ball.
Each bubble is laughing, as they float on by,
And I'm just here wondering, why did I try?

A sailboat is giggling, with no chance to steer,
While seagulls are plotting my next meal of fear.
I pause for a moment, take a breath of pure air,
And wonder if swimming is best done with flair.

So here's to the ocean, with tides that will tease,
To the beaches of laughter, the gaps in between.
Even when sinking, this dance feels so fine,
In the heart of absurd, I'll claim that I shine.

Reflections in a Shattered Mirror

In shards of this mirror, I see bits of me,
Some days I'm a hero, some days just a bee.
The glitter's a bummer, it gets in my eye,
Like confetti from parties that don't even fly.

I skip down the street, with mismatched my shoes,
Each step is a story, a whim to amuse.
I wave to my shadow, though it never waves back,
And together we giggle, plotting our track.

The world's full of nonsense, I can tell you that,
I just tripped on my thoughts, and landed in chat.
With each broken image, I laugh in delight,
In a landscape of chaos, I find my own light.

So here's to reflections, in glass that won't mend,
To the puzzles of moments, with each twist and bend.
In the realm of absurd, where kooky is king,
I'll dance like a fool, and just let it swing.

www.ingramcontent.com/pod-product-compliance
Lightning Source LLC
Chambersburg PA
CBHW051638160426
43209CB00004B/702